A souvenir guide

Tredegar House

Newport

Ymddiriedolaeth Genedlaethol
National Trust

Tredegar and the Morgans

Tredegar House was home to the Morgan family (later Lords Tredegar) for over 500 years. The fortunes of house and family were intimately connected. The impressive 1670s mansion that we see today was built around a more modest Tudor house. The site was originally chosen because of the spring that runs beneath it.

Who were the Morgans?

The Morgans were a very proud Welsh family, who claimed descent from the great Welsh princes. They were hugely influential on the political, social and economic life of Newport and in the counties of Brecon, Glamorgan and Monmouth. The Tredegar Estate once covered 53,000 acres in south-east Wales beyond Brecon and into Cardiff.

Now set in 90 acres of parkland, the house has been home to industrialists, fifteen High Sheriffs, 22 MPs, a military hero and happy family life. It has also known wild parties, lunacy and the occult. The Morgans are remembered in the portraits which hang on the walls and watch us as we explore their home. Just as important are the stories of those who worked below stairs, in the grounds and on the estate.

The house

In 1403 Llewellyn ap Morgan, who owned an estate including this site, lost much land as a punishment for supporting Owain Glyndŵr's rebellion. His descendants recovered their lands, and added more, through the 15th century. John ap Morgan's support of Henry Tudor in 1485 established the Morgans as a powerful gentry family in south-east Wales. The Tudor house (the primary roof timbers

Above The core of the earlier Tudor house can still be seen in the inner courtyard. The pump in the centre of the courtyard was fed by a spring that flows beneath

Left The south-east front

Opposite The Servants' Ball. Tredegar House has stories to tell above and below stairs

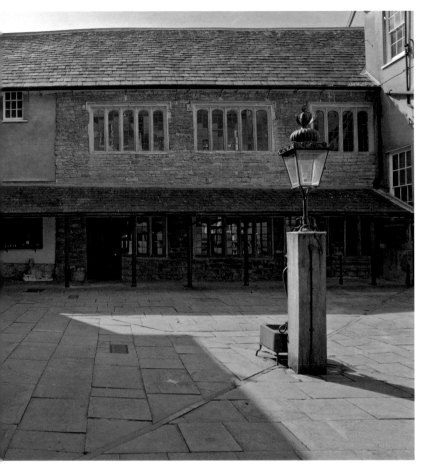

Ruperra Castle

Ruperra Castle (now in private hands) was another Morgan residence, about six miles away, which dates from 1626. From the late 18th century, when the Tredegar and Ruperra Estates were brought together, it was where the heir lived. It was sold in 1935 and gutted by fire in 1941 while soldiers were being billeted there. It remains a shell.

Ruperra Castle appears in the background of this portrait of Frederick Morgan

date from the mid-16th century) was built to reflect their new status, and was where King Charles I stayed the night in 1645. That building was of cheap, readily available grey stone, and was largely replaced by the present red-brick mansion between 1664–74. Rather than facing inwards onto an inner courtyard like the old building, the windows of the new Tredegar House looked out over the gardens and parkland.

Red brick was rarely used in South Wales in the mid-17th century, and never on this scale. Such a comparatively crisp, red building would have been unlike anything else in the area. With its grand façade and lavish interior, this was a house designed to impress.

The Morgans of Tredegar

'Tredegar House is one of the grandest and most exuberant country houses in [Wales], and one of the outstanding houses of the Restoration period in the whole of Britain.'

John Newman

A new Tredegar House

It is thought that the house was rebuilt in the red brick you see today for William Morgan (d.1680). He inherited the original house in 1666 and certainly had the financial means to carry out the work. In 1661 he had married his cousin Blanche Morgan, the only daughter of Judge William Morgan, who was the King's Attorney for South Wales and very wealthy. The money and lands that the marriage settlement brought would have helped fund the impressive Tredegar House building programme. Blanche died in 1673, and three years later William married another woman of wealth, Elizabeth Dayrell, a widow who brought even more land to the family. The estate was booming, and the Morgans were rich and fashionable – and that was the message they wanted their new house to convey. A manor house was no longer good enough for them; they wanted a red-brick mansion enriched with finely carved stone decoration.

Below left The Master's Bedchamber

Below William Morgan's second wife, Elizabeth Dayrell, who was also wealthy; artist unknown

Monkey business

Stories abound about Elizabeth Dayrell physically and verbally attacking her husband. On one occasion she went into the Master's Bedchamber, pulled back the curtains of his bed and declared to two maid servants how like a monkey he looked. Violent attacks followed, as she declared 'she would either kill or be killed'. Elizabeth was eventually declared a lunatic.

Far left Elizabeth Windham Morgan and her son William, who probably built the new house; artist unknown

Left The heiress Blanche Morgan, who married William Morgan in 1661; artist unknown, mid-17th century

A fashionable couple

When William died, Thomas (d. 1700) – his oldest son with Blanche – inherited, followed by their fourth son John. John was also heir to the fortune of his uncle, John the Merchant. In 1719 the combined fortune passed to William Morgan (1700–31), MP for Monmouthshire. William was a frivolous and fun-loving character, who spent money on fancy wigs, silver punch bowls, a racecourse at Cardiff, a cockpit at Newport and stables at Newmarket. His peacock-like behaviour attracted attention, and in 1724 he married Lady Rachel Cavendish, daughter of the 2nd Duke of Devonshire, who provided a dowry of £20,000.

William lived fast and died young – aged only 31. Lady Rachel had been promised £2000 a year in the event of her husband's death, and she lived another 50 years. This promise nearly bankrupted the family. The marriage settlement had been a complicated one, but when their only son (William) died, Rachel and her daughter Elizabeth fought Rachel's brother-in-law (Thomas Morgan of Ruperra) through the Court of Chancery to gain the estate. They lost, Thomas inherited, and the Ruperra and Tredegar Estates were brought together. Of his three sons, the last, John, died childless in 1792.

Below left Sir William Morgan; artist unknown, c.1725

Below Lady Rachel Cavendish, who married Sir William Morgan in 1724; by Charles Jervas, c.1725-30

The Morgans and the Industrial Revolution

John's eldest sister, Jane, had married Charles Gould in 1758. Because of the legal wrangling over inheritance that the family had known in recent years, John had made it clear that Charles should inherit the estate, including some 40,000 acres – providing he took the name Morgan. Charles was an impressive and ambitious character, variously appointed Judge-Advocate General, Chancellor of Salisbury, Chamberlain of Brecknock, Radnor and Glamorgan, and MP for the Borough of Brecon. He was knighted in 1779 and made a baronet in 1792, when he assumed the surname and arms of Morgan – thus ensuring the continuation of the Morgan family name.

As the Industrial Revolution transformed South Wales, the Morgans recognised the commercial potential of their land in Monmouthshire, Brecon and Glamorgan. In addition to his successful legal career, Charles invested money in financial, industrial and commercial projects, exploiting the mineral wealth of his extensive estate. The Morgan family did not own coal mines or iron works themselves, but they leased land for such projects. He also established the Monmouthshire and Brecon Canal, and shrewdly encouraged the construction of a tramroad from Sirhowy to Newport. The section that passed through Tredegar Park became known as the Golden Mile because of the profits made from tolls levied by the estate.

Left Sir Charles Gould Morgan; by William Hoare of Bath, late 18th century

Sir Charles Morgan: the impudent philanthropist

Charles Gould Morgan was succeeded in 1806 by his eldest son, Sir Charles Morgan (1760–1846). Another man of importance and influence, he too became an MP, for Brecon and Monmouthshire. He also made a substantial contribution to the development of Newport. Amongst other achievements he set up the Tredegar Wharf Company which developed Pillgwenlly marshland for housing. He also encouraged the construction of the docks and the opening of the cattle market.

Sir Charles Morgan's income at this time was over £40,000 per annum. However, while industrialists were lining their pockets, social unrest was growing. In 1830 the Chartist John Frost wrote a pamphlet, *A Christmas Box for Sir Charles Morgan*, accusing him of treating his tenants badly and calling for universal suffrage and the secret ballot as the only way to curb the power of such privileged landowners as Sir Charles: 'The people of the whole world are determined to be free; they are determined no longer to be kept in bonds by impudent and arrogant men.'

Sir Charles was also a philanthropist. He gave food, coal and blankets to the poor on his estate, and was said to have set up soup kitchens. Perhaps influenced by his friend, Lady Llanover, he promoted the Welsh language and culture, patronising harpists, and supporting the revival of the National Eisteddfod.

Tredegar House itself was the scene of extravagant celebrations during Sir Charles's time. Christmas festivities would start with the November shoots, and continue well into January. There would be huge dinners, masquerade balls and plays in which the family and their guests would have a role. There could be over 100 people in residence on such occasions, but where they all slept is a mystery.

Above Sir Charles Morgan and his family in the New Hall about 1830

Left The Chartist riot in Newport in 1839

Below Sir Charles Morgan; by Henry Pickersgill

The old man in the square
A statue of Sir Charles Morgan stands in the centre of Newport, on Bridge Street. For over 100 years it was situated in Park Square, where residents told stories of the 'old man in the square' getting up off his plinth and walking about in the night. Now his statue is situated outside the Westgate Hotel, ironically opposite a sculpture commemorating the 150th anniversary of the Newport Chartist uprising.

Finally a peer!

Sir Charles Morgan was succeeded by his son Charles Morgan Robinson Morgan in 1846. Robinson Morgan married Rosamund Mundy, who bore him eleven children. It is believed he had other illegitimate children. An eminent Victorian, he was also an MP and High Sheriff. He continued the industrial development his father and grandfather had begun, and took a keen interest in agriculture. In 1859 he was made the 1st Lord Tredegar as a reward for his support of Disraeli, who wrote of a visit to Tredegar: 'Lord Tredegar is a Welch prince with a flowing hospitality, his hall full of his neighbours; the Welch squires from their castles, unceasing hunting and fishing in a thousand torrents.'

Left Charles Morgan Robinson Morgan; artist unknown, c.1859

Godfrey the Good

Lord Tredegar's eldest son, Charles Rodney, died in 1854 aged only 25, and so he was succeeded by his younger son, Godfrey, in 1875. Godfrey had been commissioned into the 17th Lancers in 1849 and with his younger brother Frederick served in the Crimean War. Godfrey was one of only two officers from his regiment to come unscathed through the Charge of the Light Brigade in October 1854. He had become engaged before he left for the Crimea, but while he was away, his fiancée married another man. Godfrey never married.

Godfrey's position as head of the house came with responsibilities. A Conservative MP, when his father died, he ascended to the House of Lords. He held many other positions including Lord Lieutenant of Monmouthshire and of Breconshire, and he was a magistrate for Breconshire and Glamorgan. In 1905 Godfrey became Viscount Tredegar and in 1909 he was made a freemen of Newport and Cardiff. He enjoyed cricket and bowls, ensuring that Tredegar House had both a bowling green and a cricket pitch. A very visible presence in the area, Godfrey much preferred life at Tredegar House to London society.

Godfrey was also remembered for his great generosity. As befitted a wealthy man of the period, he was a public benefactor and

Right Equestrian portrait of Godfrey Morgan with Tredegar House in the background. Huntsman Charles Barrett is on the horse behind him; by John Charlton, 1884

Below *The Charge of the Light Brigade*; by John Charlton, 1905

philanthropist. He gave land to create Belle View Park, the Royal Gwent Hospital, the Athletic Ground in Newport, and University College in Cardiff. He reduced rents in times of hardship, and when a young woman on the estate was widowed, he let her stay rent-free for the rest of her life. Recognising the esteem in which Godfrey was held, a Labour leader said publicly 'that Socialism would not flourish at Newport so long as Lord Tredegar was alive'.

Very proud of his Welsh lineage, he commissioned the Hirlas Horn, an integral part of the National Eisteddfod, and presented it to the Archdruid in 1899. He also played Owain Glyndŵr, the last Welshman to be Prince of Wales, in the National Pageant of Wales in 1909. This was regarded as one national hero playing another: 'It is with great interest that such a loyal and notable Welsh

Soldier as Viscount Tredegar … should to-day be appearing in the rôle of the famous rebel warrior who led his own people so successfully against the English.'

Godfrey was the most popular of the Morgans. When he died in 1913, the Estate was at its peak: the *South Wales Argus* estimated that his income was £1000 a day. The viscountcy became extinct on his death, and the barony and baronetcy passed to his nephew, Courtenay Morgan (1867–1934). There were also heavy death-duties to be paid.

Sir Briggs – a heroic horse for a heroic man
Sir Briggs was named after Bridger Champion, who had served as Godfrey Morgan's 'batman' (personal servant) at Aldershot, and became head groomsman at Ruperra Castle. Sir Briggs was the charger that Godfrey took out to the Crimea, and rode in the Charge of the Light Brigade. Both were lucky to survive. Sir Briggs returned to Tredegar and when he died, was buried in the Cedar Garden beneath an obelisk.

The last of the Morgans of Tredegar House

Courtenay was born and grew up at Ruperra Castle. He spent vast amounts on mistresses, on hunting, shooting and fishing, and on his yachts, the largest of which was the *Liberty*. Courtenay is said to have sailed her twice around the world. At the outbreak of World War I he paid for her to be fitted out as a hospital ship.

Courtenay was the archetypal country gentleman, but the world was changing around him. He married Lady Katharine Carnegie, daughter of the Earl of Southesk, in 1890. She spent little time at Tredegar House, preferring to live in south-east England. They had two children, Evan and Gwyneth, who were bright young things of the 1920s. Experimenting with all the good, bad and bohemian of the time may have led to Gwyneth's death. In 1925, when she was only 29, her body was found in the Thames. There were rumours of links to drug dens.

Bright young things

Evan succeeded Courtenay in 1934, and it is about him that some of the most intriguing and scandalous stories are told.

A man with great wealth, he looked for ways to occupy his time. Bad health put paid to a commission with the Welsh Guards. He tried poetry and painting, and Tredegar House was

Below left Courtenay, Viscount Tredegar dressed as a captain in the Royal Naval Volunteer Reserve; by Movat Loudan, 1920

Below centre Katharine, Viscountess Tredegar; by Augustus John, c.1920. Although they are rumoured to have had an affair, when painting this portrait, John said, 'I am painting Lady Tredegar ... a trying subject, but will pay up'

Below right Evan, Viscount Tredegar in Papal garb; by Cathleen Mann, 1941

Evan concealed his homosexuality beneath two marriages of convenience. The first was to Lois Sturt, an actress and heiress. Her family was keen for her to marry, as she had had a long affair with Reggie Herbert, the (married) Earl of Pembroke. She agreed to marry Evan, who was a friend. She died of a heart attack, in 1937 aged 37, when a guest of the Cartiers in Budapest. Two years later he married the White Russian émigré Princess Olga Dolgorouky. She spent time training with the St John Ambulance and nursed in Newport. Olga wrote that Evan used to have 'great flights of fancy at times and I never knew what was fact or fiction'. The marriage was annulled in 1943, but they remained friends.

Evan was the last Morgan to live at Tredegar. When he died in 1949, the titles passed to his uncle Frederick, who immediately transferred the estates to his son John to avoid a third imposition of death-duties. Even so, John felt unable to cope with the financial burden of the house, so sold up and moved to the South of France. He died in 1962, and was the last of the Morgans of Tredegar.

infamous for wild weekend parties with mixed nude bathing in the lake. He was friends with many of the leading artistic figures of the era, from Jacob Epstein to Charlie Chaplin, Augustus John to Nancy Cunard, Aldous Huxley to H.G. Wells. Another friend was Aleister Crowley, 'the Beast'. Evan had converted to Catholicism, and served as a Privy Chamberlain at the Vatican, but he was also an occultist.

The Tredegar House Zoo

Evan had a menagerie of animals, many of which would roam the house and grounds. They included a kangaroo called Somerset, Alice the honeybear, and a baboon named Bimbo. Maybe through his mother's influence he had an aviary, and trained a cockatiel to run up his trouser leg and appear through his flies! Blue Boy, his macaw, was well known among the servants for its bad language, while the baboon once got into the Housekeeper's Room and caused no end of damage. It wasn't just exotic pets that Evan accommodated. He used to sleep with rabbits in his bed, much to the dismay of the maids who had to clean up!

Above Evan Morgan with his macaw Blue Boy in 1933

Exploring Tredegar House

'The House of the Morgans at Tredegar is equal only to Powis among the great houses of Wales.'

Simon Jenkins

The 1670s red-brick house we see today makes a dramatic statement about the power, wealth and taste of the Morgan family. Catching sight of the monumental Tredegar House from afar, approaching through the imposing gates, and entering the candle-lit interior must have been an experience to inspire and intimidate. But despite the house's importance, we do not know who designed it, nor who was responsible for the superb quality of its interior craftsmanship.

The Ground Floor

The lavishness of the exterior continues inside with the intricately decorated state rooms. The New Hall, Dining Room and Gilt Room remain the most elaborate spaces. Originally, the family would not have used these rooms on a day-to-day basis, but for occasional grand displays. Guests would have paraded through the New Hall, dined in the Dining Room, and retired to enjoy further entertainment in the Gilt Room. As with the exterior, many foreign styles are brought together. The Mannerist carvings in the Dining Room show extraordinary skill, with playful detail everywhere you look. The Gilt Room impresses with its fireplace, not unlike an Italian Baroque altarpiece. The cheap pine panels are grained

Above The Side Hall

Left The Gilt Room: 'one of the great rooms of Wales' (Simon Jenkins)

Below A carved beast in the Dining Room

Prize possessions

The Cedar Closet was where the master would have kept his most important documents and clothes – cedar being a natural moth repellent. Upon closer inspection, the cedar wood is revealed to be only a veneer: the Morgans cut costs by constructing the majority of the closet from cheaper wood. The glass-fronted cabinet, a cabinet of curiosities, would have been used to display treasured objects, a precursor to today's museums.

house, whilst the third corner housed the Master's Bedchamber. The last and most intimate room of this last suite was the Cedar Closet, where only the master's very closest friends would have been admitted.

A life after the Morgans

The house didn't leave the Morgan family until 1951, when it was sold, with most of its contents and surrounding estates, to the Sisters of St Joseph. For 23 years Tredegar House was a school, first for girls with some boarding in the former servants' quarters in the attics, and then a state comprehensive. It is hard to imagine such grand rooms being used as classrooms or offices. Newport Borough Council bought the house and the surrounding land in 1974. Thanks to the foresight of some, it was decided that it should become a historic house museum, and the gradual process of restoring and refurbishing began. Fortunately, about a third of the items on display today are original. Some are part of the permanent collection, while others are loans from private individuals and national institutions. They range from family portraits to pots and pans, and even rabbit traps from the estate. The house has become popular for many events including school workshops, weddings and filming – with Dr Who being a frequent visitor!

In March 2012 the National Trust acquired Tredegar House on a 50-year lease.

to imitate more desirable walnut. The ceiling and the wall panels are decorated with paintings copied from the Palazzo Barberini in Rome, and Amsterdam Town Hall.

In Victorian times the Side Hall was introduced as the main entrance, with the New Parlour becoming the family dining room.

The First Floor

In the late 17th-century building, the first floor was divided into three separate suites. The Best Chamber was in one corner, where the favoured guest would have been disturbed the least. Another corner suite would traditionally have been reserved for the mistress of the

Below The Best Chamber was set aside for honoured guests

Below right The unrestored School Rroom

Life below stairs

Above **The bells**

Left **The Great Kitchen**

Below **The spice cupboard. The keys to the cupboard would be kept by the Housekeeper. This symbolised her authority over the cook, who would have to come and ask for the more expensive ingredients**

When the red-brick house was built, a division between family and servants' areas not previously so pronounced was starting to appear. Servants should be neither seen nor heard. Today, it is hard to imagine the noise and smells that would have emanated from the Great Kitchen, where the six or so staff could be busy preparing as many as eight courses for the Morgans and their guests.

The number of staff varied depending on who was living here, but in the mid-19th century there were 45 servants in the house, with a similar number in both the grounds and at Home Farm. Jobs ranged from house steward (head of the male servants), housekeeper (head of the female servants – often unmarried, but always called 'Mrs' as a sign of seniority), kitchen helper, valet, poultry maid, hall maid, housemaid, kitchen maid, dairy maid, laundry maid, blacksmith, lodgekeeper, cowman, woodman, haulier, carpenter, electrical engineer and miller.

The Morgan family may have had the longest association with Tredegar House, but there were also dynasties below stairs, for example the Hazells and Barretts, who are also immortalised in paintings. Their families still return to Tredegar House to share memories. The servants and estate workers were essential to the running of the house, estate and the Morgan lifestyle. Tredegar House was a real community where people met their future spouses, and children grew up together on the estate. The estate sports teams included rugby, hockey and cricket, with lemonade, cakes and sandwiches being brought out for the spectators.

Working days may have been long, perhaps from 6am to 8pm, with many servants busy in the evenings too, when the Morgans were in residence. But conditions were good, with food and lodgings provided. It was a very different type of servitude to that experienced by those working in industry.

Above **Servants in the courtyard**

Above right **The Servants' Ball**

The relationship between those below stairs and those above varied greatly, but Godfrey and Evan seem to have got on best with their servants.

The Servants' Ball

The Servants' Ball at Tredegar House was famous in the area. Although it varied, usually it was held on the Friday closest to Twelfth Night, 6 January. Lord Tredegar and his party would be there for the start, when he would dance with the Housekeeper. Dance cards would be provided, and a hired band would play until 6am, when the servants had to start work again. Estate workers and local suppliers were also invited. No expense would be spared on the food, which was described as being 'out of this world'. It would include lobster, mayonnaises of salmon, veal, jellies, cake, trifles and tarts – and enough drink to wash it all down!

The Outbuildings

Tredegar House was self-sufficient, and many outbuildings were essential to the operation. We still have the workshops, the cattle byre, the mill and barns. The most impressive are the Stables and Orangery. These were probably built in the late 17th century by Thomas Morgan, son of the William Morgan responsible for rebuilding the house. Just like

Above **A footman in livery**

Right **The Edney Gates**

the house, they was meant to impress. The scene was completed with the addition of the wrought-iron screen and gates, bought from the Edney brothers of Bristol c.1714–18. One half of the Stables houses the stalls, the other the riding school. Apparently when Charles and Diana visited, the chauffeur drove them to the Stables, thinking that was the entrance to the house!

The Orangery was also a status symbol: expensive to build and maintain – as were the fruit trees, including orange and lemons, that it housed. The Tredegar Orangery faces south-west, so the vast windows make maximum use of all available light. In addition, the Orangery was originally heated through hot-air ducts concealed in the floor and rear wall which were fed from a boiler below.

The Gardens and Park

The formal walled gardens are split into three enclosures linked by one large central gravel path. The original garden, probably Tudor, was redesigned in the early 1700s, not long after the red-brick house was rebuilt and in the same red brick. Like the Tudor garden, they were still very formal, but introduced wide gravel walks, parterres, fountains and statues, inspired by the grand Baroque gardens of Europe.

The Orchard Garden

The largest of the three enclosures contained the orchard, the Head Gardener's cottage, the Agent's office and other garden buildings and offices. In Victorian times the gardens developed further with the installation of glasshouses. The kitchen garden, which had consisted of several acres, was elsewhere on site. It has since been built on – first by St Josephs school, when it left Tredegar House, and now by a housing estate.

The Cedar Garden

The middle enclosure is the Cedar Garden, dominated by a cedar of Lebanon. Within the central yew hedge is Sir Briggs's obelisk (p.9).

The Orangery Garden

Excavations in the late 1980s revealed an early 18th-century garden layout, with evidence of sea shells, lime mortar, brick dust, coal dust, white sand, orange sand and grass. What you see today gives a impression of how it would have looked.

The Park

The deer-park was once over 1000 acres (404 hectares). Now the deer have gone, and the park is reduced to 90 acres (32 hectares). There were oak, walnut and chestnut tree avenues, which radiated out from the house. The most prominent Oak Avenue is still visible, leading from the house, across the park, and seen continuing up to the brow of the hill beyond the M4. Adam Mickle, a landscape architect, was employed by John Morgan in 1788. His scheme was to landscape the park, by enhancing it and bringing it right up to the house, as was fashionable at the time. The removal of the formal walled gardens and the stables was proposed as part of the project, but fortunately this was not carried out. A lake was added, as was the toll road from Newport to Cardiff (now the A48), which cut the park in two long before the M4 was created.

Above **The Orangery Garden**